TOP TEN SLOWEST WONDERS ON EARTH

BY JOHN ALLAN

CONTENTS

WELCOME TO THE WORLD'S SLOWEST!	4
SLOWEST MAMMAL	6
SLOWEST GROWING TREE	8
SLOWEST PLANE	10
SLOWEST CLOUDS	12
SLOWEST CAR	14
SLOWEST MUSIC	16
SLOWEST FLYING BIRD	18
SLOWEST TRAIN	20
SLOWEST FISH	22
SLOWEST HEARTBEAT	24
SLOWEST THING IN OUTER SPACE	26
CLOSE, BUT NOT CLOSE ENOUGH!	28
THE PEOPLE BEHIND THE RECORDS	30
GLOSSARY	31
INDEX	32

Copyright © 2025 Hungry Tomato Ltd

First published in 2025 by Hungry Tomato Ltd
F15, Old Bakery Studios, Blewetts Wharf, Malpas Road, Truro, Cornwall, TR1 1QH, UK.

No part of this publication may be reproduced, stored in a retrieval system, or transmitted in any form or by any means, electronic, mechanical, photocopying, recording, or otherwise, without prior written permission of the copyright owner.

A CIP catalogue record for this book is available from the British Library.

ISBN 9781835694237

Printed in China

Discover more at
www.hungrytomato.com

Words in **BOLD** can be found in the glossary.

WELCOME TO THE WORLD'S SLOWEST!

We live on a planet with so many impressive things. Prepare to be amazed by some of the world's slowest record-breakers...

MADE BY HUMANS OR NATURE?

The slowest things in the world come in all shapes and sizes. Some are incredible animals with unique and surprising features, and others are amazing human-made machines. Can you guess which will come out on top?

MEASURING SPEED

You can usually see when something is super slow, but how can you tell exactly how slow it is? Speed is measured by working out how far a specific thing could travel in an hour. This is usually written as miles, or kilometres (km) per hour.

MAKING HISTORY

Humans are always hoping their name, and their creations, go down in history. Modern technology and our understanding of science and engineering makes this more possible every day. The machines in this book were made by incredibly talented people.

HOLDING ONTO A RECORD

People around the world are always competing to build even more complex machines to try and break records. This means that records and stats are constantly changing for human-made machines.

This book showcases 10 of the slowest things in the world!
It's hard to compare these record-breakers as they are all so different. What's slow for a machine may seem fast compared to an animal, but it's still impressive. The top 10 in this book are in no particular order, but everyone will have a favourite!

1 SLOWEST MAMMAL

Living in the tropical rainforests of South America is the world's slowest mammal, the three-toed sloth.

Sloths hang upside down in the trees, hiding within the branches and leaves. They eat, sleep, and even give birth in the trees. They move very, very slowly. When they're on the ground, their average speed is 0.07 miles per hour (0.1 km/h)!

Sloths' fur is the perfect place for fungi and algae to grow! They help sloths to stay camouflaged and out of sight from predators like eagles, ocelots, and jaguars. It also makes them smell like plants.

DID YOU KNOW?

Sloths spend about 15 hours of the day sleeping! They can even sleep while hanging from the branches of trees.

SUPER FACT

Sloths don't just move slowly – they also have very slow **metabolisms**, which means they can survive on very little food. What takes most animals a few hours to digest, it can take sloths days!

2 SLOWEST GROWING TREE

White cedar trees are known for being one of the slowest growing trees in the world, but the slowest of all was a true record-breaker.

Located on a cliffside in the Canadian Great Lakes was the world's slowest growing tree. It had only grown to a height of 10.2 cm (4 inches) in 155 years!

This tiny plant was very light, weighing only 17 grams (0.6 oz) – which meant that it had grown by 0.11 grams (0.004 oz) of wood every year on average.

DID YOU KNOW?

White cedars are evergreen trees, which means they don't lose their leaves in winter, but stay green all year round. Because of this, they are popular and often grown in parks and people's gardens. They are also loved by animals who use the trees for food and shelter.

SUPER FACT

Usually slow-growing trees live much longer than fast-growing trees. White cedar often live to be hundreds of years old, and the oldest ever recorded was thought to be more than 1,600 years old.

3 SLOWEST PLANE

It may be an unusual record, but the slowest jet aircraft in the world is the Polish PZL M-15 Belphegor.

SUPER FACT
Today, farmers don't use the word "crop-dusting", they prefer "aerial application". This is because they no longer use dust on crops, but liquids!

Belphegor is a **biplane** that was created to help with crop-dusting – spreading substances over farmland to help crops grow. It had a top speed of just 120 miles per hour (195 km/h). This may sound fast, but it's very slow in comparison with normal planes which travel closer to 600 miles per hour (965 km/h).

The Belphegor's first flight was in 1973. It is still the only jet biplane to ever go into production. Only 175 were ever built, as they were incredibly expensive to build and to use.

DID YOU KNOW?

Some farmers today prefer to use drones to apply farming substances instead of biplanes. These are easier and safer to use, and usually much cheaper to buy!

4 SLOWEST CLOUDS

We think of clouds being light and easily moved through the sky by wind, but some clouds are so slow that they don't move at all!

These clouds are called "lenticular clouds". They often form on the sheltered side of a mountain or other large geographical features, and stay still in the sky while air moves through them! They can last in one place for several hours at a time.

They form at high **altitudes** of up to 7.5 miles (12 km) and are shaped like discs. Because of their unusual, disc-like shape, they are often mistaken for UFOs!

SUPER FACT

Pilots avoid flying near lenticular clouds because the powerful waves of air that form the clouds can cause **turbulence**.

DID YOU KNOW?

Lenticular clouds can reflect sunlight and shadows in a way that makes them stand out even more in the sky!

5 SLOWEST CAR

The Peel P50 isn't just the slowest car in the world, it's also the smallest production car ever made!

The Peel P50 is a three-wheeled microcar that was first made in 1962 and was designed as a city car – it was only big enough for a driver and a shopping bag. Its top speed was 38 miles per hour (61 km/h), which is slower than some dogs can run!

This car's slow speed is down to its very small engine. Industry professionals often measure engines in **cc** – the Peel P50's engine was only 49cc, which is the same size as engines found in **mopeds**.

DID YOU KNOW?

The original model didn't have a reversing gear! But a small handle at the back of the car allowed it to be moved by pushing and pulling when needed – it was light enough for people to do this!

SUPER FACT

Because of its engine size and speed, some countries don't class the Peel P50 as a car, calling it a moped or quadricycle instead!

6 SLOWEST MUSIC

An unusual record to try and achieve, the world's longest and slowest piece of music is still being played in Germany.

The music was written by an American composer named John Cage. He called the music "As Slow As Possible". A group of musicians are helping to make the piece of music last for 639 years!

The piece of music, which is being played on an organ, began in 2001, almost 10 years after its composer passed away. Each chord or note lasts for months at a time. To keep the note playing for so long, weights are put on the organ pedals. The final note is due to be played in the year 2640.

DID YOU KNOW?

This music is being played in Halberstadt, Germany, where the world's first large organ was built. In the year 2000, it had been 639 years since the organ's creation, which is why this song is going to be that long!

SUPER FACT
The weights keep a single organ note playing for months at a time!

7 SLOWEST FLYING BIRD

The slowest flying birds in the world are both woodcocks – the American and the Eurasian woodcocks share this record.

Small, but memorable, these birds perform "sky dances" when trying to find a **mate**, flying in complex patterns to try and catch other birds' attention. They have been recorded flying as slow as 5 miles per hour (8 km/h) during these performances!

When **migrating**, they can fly faster, but usually stay at low altitudes and only for short distances at a time. Scientists think this is because they have short wings and round bodies.

DID YOU KNOW?

Woodcocks spend most of their time on the ground in forests, where they make nests. They are impressive survivors: their feathers **camouflage** them against the ground, their big eyes help them watch for danger, and they use their long **bills** to grab worms from the soil.

SUPER FACT

The American woodcock has lots of names – some people also call it the timberdoodle, night partridge, and bog sucker!

8 SLOWEST TRAIN

The Glacier Express is known as "the slowest express train in the world". It travels at an average speed of 24 miles per hour (39 km/h).

The Glacier Express is in Switzerland and travels between the towns of St Moritz and Zermatt. The train's eight-hour journey takes passengers through the stunning Swiss Alps; its slow pace is perfect for admiring the view of the mountains and valleys.

The train's first journey took place in 1930. The train is still in operation today. It's estimated that more than 200,000 people ride on the Glacier Express every year!

DID YOU KNOW?

The Glacier Express isn't the only train to take passengers from St Moritz to Zermatt, but its slower speed and extra-large windows are a huge attraction for tourists wanting to take in the scenery.

SUPER FACT

The Glacier Express' journey goes through 91 tunnels and over 291 bridges.

9 SLOWEST FISH

The slowest fish in the world is also the smallest animal in this book! This record goes to the seahorse.

There are more than 30 **species** of seahorse, all of them extremely slow swimmers. The slowest of all is the dwarf seahorse, which scientists think never moves faster than 0.001 miles per hour (0.016 km/h).

Dwarf seahorses are tiny, growing up to a maximum height of only 4.2 cm (1.7 inches). Their slow swimming speed is because their bodies are very **rigid** and they lack a tail fin. The **dorsal fin** on their back is quick, but small compared to the body.

DID YOU KNOW?

Seahorses can't swim against the current. To stop themselves from being swept away, they use their tails to hold onto seaweed and other plants!

SUPER FACT

Seahorses don't have teeth or a stomach! They eat tiny fish and **crustaceans**, which they suck in with their long snouts. They have to eat lots to stay alive.

23

10 SLOWEST HEARTBEAT

They may be the biggest and most majestic animals on the planet, but blue whales are also believed to be the mammal with the slowest heartbeat!

Blue whales' hearts usually only beat between 4 and 8 times per minute, but scientists have recorded them dropping as low as twice per minute when whales dive deeper in search of food. Scientists think whales slow their heartbeats to save oxygen and energy as they dive.

SUPER FACT

Blue whales have the largest hearts of any living animal — these impressively powerful **organs** can weigh the same as an upright piano.

Even when they are at the surface, the blue whale's heartbeat only gets as high as 37 beats per minute – which is still very slow! This is a huge difference from the average resting human heartbeat, which is between 60 and 100 beats per minute.

DID YOU KNOW?

Blue whales are record-breaking animals all around, being the biggest and heaviest overall, having the largest eyes, lungs, and heart, among other amazing features.

SLOWEST THINGS IN OUTER SPACE

You've now heard about 10 of the slowest things in the world. But what about the slowest things in outer space?

SLOWEST PLANET

All the planets in our solar system spin, but Venus spins the slowest. It takes Earth 23 hours and 56 minutes to complete one spin – what we call a "day" – but Venus takes 243 "Earth days" to complete one spin! Because it's so close to the Sun, a year on Venus is much quicker than a day!

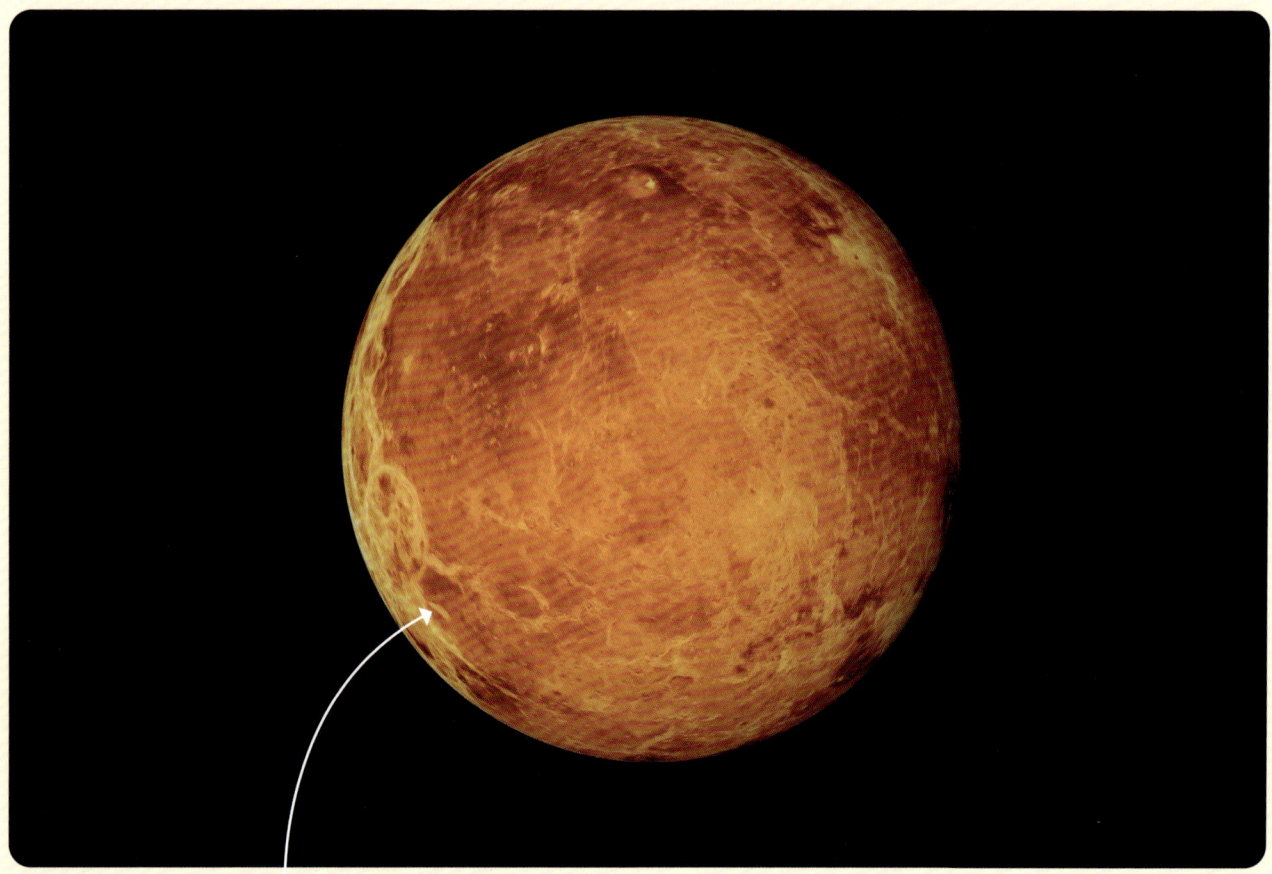

VENUS IS THE SECOND-CLOSEST PLANET TO OUR SUN.

SLOWEST STAR

Stars spin too! The slowest discovered to date is a **neutron star**. This type of star usually takes a second, or even less, to complete one spin, but scientists have found one that takes 54 minutes to complete one spin! They have named it ASKAP J1935+2148.

NEUTRON STARS ARE THE REMAINS OF A DEAD STAR!

SLOWEST BLACK HOLE

Scientists have discovered a pair of black holes in a distant **galaxy** called 0402+379, which are **orbiting** each other, incredibly slowly. It's estimated that it will take the black holes 30,000 years to complete one orbit of each other! This is the first time scientists have ever measured this process.

BLACK HOLES ARE SO POWERFUL THAT NOTHING, NOT EVEN LIGHT, CAN ESCAPE ONCE INSIDE!

CLOSE, BUT NOT CLOSE ENOUGH!

There are lots of impressively slow things on Earth that didn't quite make our top ten. Here are some incredible runners-up.

SLOWEST CONSTRUCTION PROJECT

The Great Wall of China is thought to be the slowest construction project in history. It took about 2,000 years to be built! It's also the longest structure ever built by humans.

SLOWEST-FLOWERING PLANT

A rare species of giant bromeliad called Puya raimondii is the slowest-flowering plant in the world. It doesn't produce flowers until between 80 and 150 years into its life. After flowering once, the plant dies!

SLOWEST MARATHON

Shizo Kanakuri holds the record for slowest Olympic marathon. He started it in 1912 but didn't finish it until 1967 – 54 years, 246 days, and 5 hours later – because he collapsed in the 1912 run and had to withdraw.

SLOWEST INSECT WING BEAT

The European swallowtail butterfly has the slowest wing beat of any insect. It beats its wings 300 times per minute. In comparison, the fastest insect wing beat record belongs to a midge at 62,760 beats per minute!

SLOWEST-AGEING ANIMAL

Greenland sharks are one of the slowest-ageing animals. They live for hundreds of years – the oldest Greenland shark recorded was around 400 years old. They can't make baby sharks until they're at least 150 years old.

THE PEOPLE BEHIND THE RECORDS

Humans have made some incredible, record-breaking things throughout history. Here's just some of the people behind the amazing records in this book.

JOHN CAGE

John Cage, the composer of the world's slowest piece of music was known for his unusual use of musical instruments. His other famous piece is 4'33", a piece where musicians don't play their instruments at all!

CYRIL CANNEL & HENRY KISSACK

The original model of the Peel P50, the world's slowest car, was designed and built by Cyril Cannel & Henry Kissack. It was first launched in 1962! The design was updated around 2010 by new company owners.

KAZIMIERZ GOCYŁA AND RIAMIR IZMAILOV

The design for the world's slowest jet plane was created by lead designers and engineers, Kazimierz Gocyła and Riamir Izmailov, who based it on the An-2 plane.

GLOSSARY

Altitudes – the distance of an object above a surface. Aircraft altitude is usually measured in comparison with sea level.

Bills (bird) – the bony mouthpiece that comes out of a bird's face.

Biplane – a plane with two main supporting surfaces placed one above the other.

Camouflage – the way animals blend in with their surroundings so they can't be seen easily.

Cc – this number refers to the size of a vehicle's engine. The bigger the cc, the more powerful the engine.

Crustaceans – animals with a hard shell and several pairs of legs that usually live in water. Crabs and lobsters are crustaceans.

Dorsal fin – a fin that is on an animal's back.

Galaxy – a huge collection of gas, dust, stars, and planets. The Milky Way is the galaxy that Earth is in.

Mate – one of a pair of animals that live or have babies together.

Metabolism – the process a living body uses to break down and digest food, and turn it into energy.

Migrating – when animals move from one place to another, usually to find food or because of changes in the weather.

Mopeds – lightweight, low-powered motorbikes.

Neutron star – a space object made of the remains of a dead star.

Orbiting – when a space object follows a repeated path to circle around another object in space.

Organ (body part) – part of a living body that has a specific job to do. For example, the heart is an organ that pumps blood around the body.

Rigid – stiff and inflexible.

Species – a group of living things that share characteristics and features.

Tropical rainforests – forests that are very hot and wet, and the plants grow closely together. They are usually found near the equator.

Turbulence – when a plane hits a strong wind current that pushes or pulls it. This makes the plane ride feel bumpy for a short time.

INDEX

A
American woodcock 18-19
ASKAP J1935+2148 (star) 27
As Slow As Possible (music) 16-17, 30

B
Black hole 27
Blue whale 24-25

C
Cage, John 16, 30
Cannel, Cyril 30

E
Eurasian woodcock 18
European swallowtail butterfly 29

G
Galaxy 0402+379 27
Glacier Express train 20-21
Gocyła, Kazimierz 30
Great Lakes, Canada 8

Great Wall of China, China 28
Greenland shark 29

H
Halberstadt, Germany 16

I
Izmailov, Riamir 30

K
Kanakuri, Shizo 29
Kissack, Henry 30

L
Lenticular clouds 12-13

M
Midge 29

N
Neutron star 27

O
Olympic marathon 29

P
Peel P50 (car) 14-15, 30
Polish PZL M-15 Belphegor 10-11, 30
Puya raimondii (plant) 28

T
Three-toed sloth 6-7
Tropical rainforests 6-7, 31

S
Seahorse 22-23
South America 6-7
Swiss Alps, Switzerland 20-21

V
Venus (planet) 26

W
White cedar 8-9

Picture credits:
Abbreviations: m-middle, t-top, l-left, r-right, bg-background.

Wikipedia: By User:VargaA - Own work, CC BY-SA 4.0, https://commons.wikimedia.org/w/index.php?curid=11604313 1bg, 10-11bg, 30bl; By MrWalkr - Own work, CC BY-SA 4.0, https://commons.wikimedia.org/w/index.php?curid=150998465 5l, 15bg, 30mr; By No machine-readable author provided. Wikipedia-ce assumed (based on copyright claims). - No machine-readable source provided. Own work assumed (based on copyright claims)., Public Domain, https://commons.wikimedia.org/w/index.php?curid=498898 17bg; By Bogaerts, Rob / Anefo - Fotocollectie Anefo. Nationaal Archief, Den Haag, nummertoegang 2.24.01.05, bestanddeelnummer 934-2728., CC0, https://commons.wikimedia.org/w/index.php?curid=40939081 30tl; By andreboeni - https://www.flickr.com/photos/65344061@N06/37750463295/, CC BY 2.0, https://commons.wikimedia.org/w/index.php?curid=110179353 14br; By Unknown author (Asahi Shinbun) - [1], Public Domain, https://commons.wikimedia.org/w/index.php?curid=40767224 29tl. NASA: images-assets.nasa.gov/image/PIA16695/PIA16695~orig.jpg 27br.

Shutterstock: 18br, 26b, 29bl; AaronChenPS2 5mr, 20-21bg; Ajit S N 24-25bg; Alex Harrigan 21mr; ARK NEYMAN 16br; Basicdog 22b, 31br; Crystaldream 9bg; Galyna Andrushko 28br; GolfX 4ml, 23bg; Henri_Lehtola 2-3bg,18-19bg; Janet Griffin 8br; Lukas Kovarik 7bg; Melnikov Dmitriy 11mr; Mikadun 13tm; Nazarii_Neshcherenskyi 27tl; Okan Ataman 6br; Sergey Uryadnikov 25mr; Thiago Oris Laranjeiras 12-13bg; Underworld 4br; Wirestock Creators 29mr; Yuri Yaunik 28ml.

Every effort has been made to trace the copyright holders, and we apologise in advance for any unintentional omissions. We would be pleased to insert the appropriate acknowledgements in any subsequent edition of this publication.